FOOTBALL LEGENDS ALPHABET

Words by Robin Feiner

A is for **A**nthony Muñoz. Arguably the best offensive tackle in recent history, Muñoz was a great player and an even greater man. Honored as NFL Man of the Year in 1991, coach Sam Wyche said of him, "That is what heroes are supposed to look like and act like."

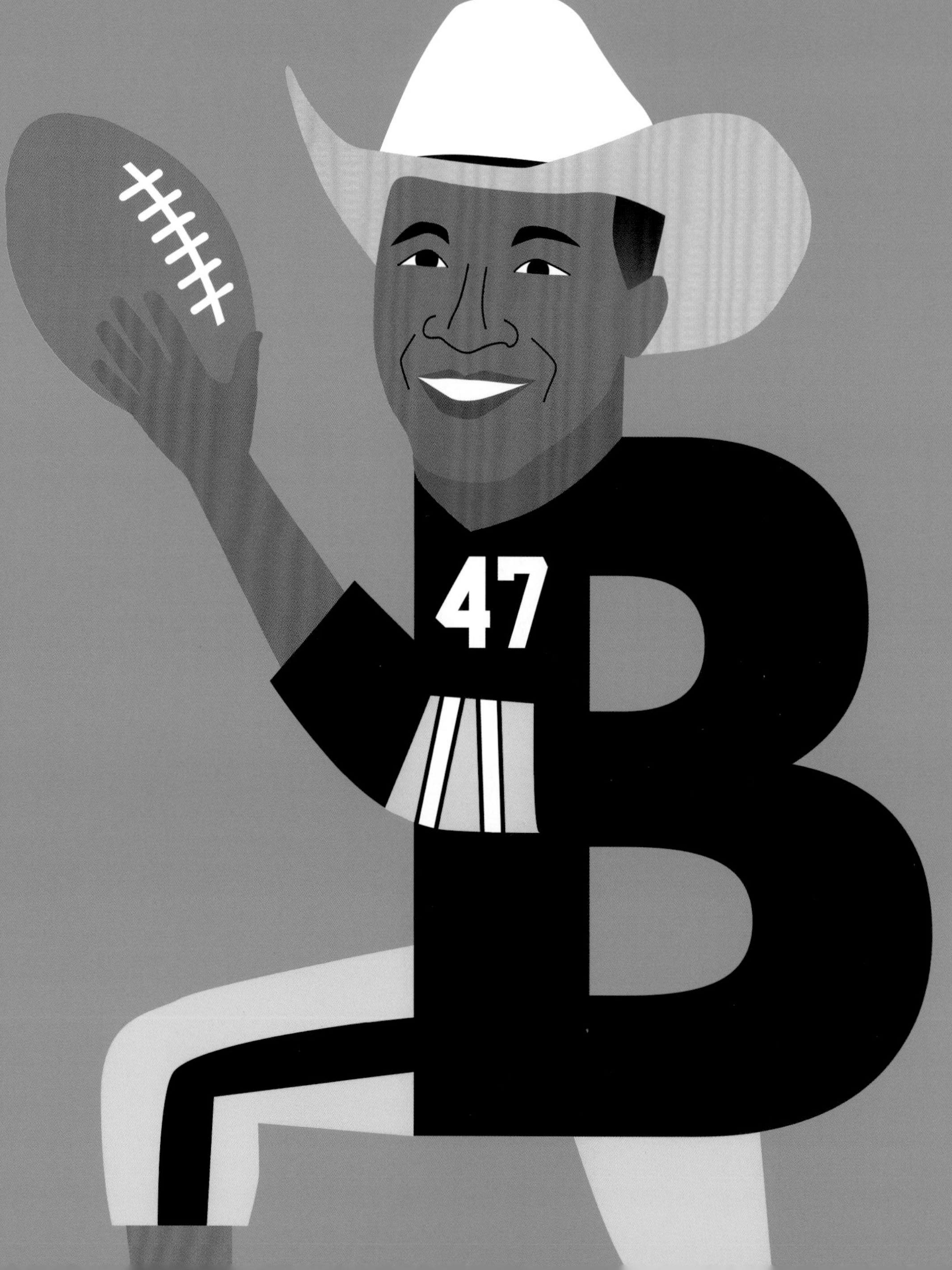
47
B

Bb

B is for Mel Blount. Considered one of the best cornerbacks of all time, Blount did more than his fair share to make the Steelers the dominant team of the 70s. Due to his intimidating, physical style of play, a rule change even became known as the Mel Blount Rule!

C is for Calvin Johnson. At 6'5" and 239 pounds, Johnson remarkably ran the 40-yard dash in 4.35 seconds! This rare combination of size and speed made 'Megatron' the most physically dominant wide receiver of all time. His 1,964 receiving yards in one season is an NFL record.

D is for Dick Butkus.
This middle linebacker to define
all linebackers was a fierce
competitor and a force on
the field. With 22 interceptions
and a record-breaking 27
fumble recoveries, Butkus was
the heart of the 'Monsters of
the Midway' defense.

E is for **E**mmitt Smith.
This Cowboys legend is the
NFL's all-time leading rusher.
He's also the only running
back to ever win a Super Bowl
championship, the NFL MVP
award, the Super Bowl MVP
award and the NFL rushing
crown all in one season!

F is for Brett Favre.
A 20-year veteran of the NFL with a legendary swathe of records, 'The Gunslinger' was the first quarterback in NFL history to pass for 500 touchdowns, throw for 70,000 yards and complete 6,000 passes. He is also the only quarterback to win three consecutive NFL MVP awards!

G is for Joe **G**reene.
As the heart of Pittsburgh's legendary 'Steel Curtain' defense, this four-time Super Bowl champion dominated the NFL in the 70s. A tough guy with a soft side, the legacy of 'Mean' Joe Greene was perfectly captured in the 'Hey Kid, Catch!' Coca-Cola commercial, which aired during Super Bowl XIV.

H is for Don **H**utson. Famous for his fast fake-outs and skillful maneuvers on every play, the 'Alabama Antelope' was a receiver ahead of his time. Inventing pass patterns in the early 1930s that are still in play today, Hutson completely revolutionized the way football is played.

I is for Michael **I**rvin.
At 6'2" and 207 pounds, Irvin was a big, physical receiver with a larger-than-life personality to match. As one of the Cowboys' key offensive players, 'The Playmaker' was renowned for making big plays during his college and pro careers.

J is for **J**erry Rice.
This legendary wide receiver is the all-time NFL leader in receptions, touchdowns and yards. With his dazzling runs leaving defenders "grasping at air and gasping for breath," it's no wonder 'Flash 80' is considered the greatest wide receiver in NFL history!

K is for Jim Kelly.
Running the 'K-Gun' no-huddle offense, 'Machine Gun Kelly' led the Bills to a record four consecutive Super Bowls. The star quarterback and his 'go-to' wide receiver, Andre Reed, connected for 65 touchdowns. They are one of the best pass combos of all time.

L is for Jack **L**ambert. After an 11-year career with the Pittsburgh Steelers, this ferocious middle linebacker was famously named by Fox Sports as the "toughest football player of all time," and "the premier linebacker of his era" by the Pro Football Hall of Fame. Legendary!

M is for Joe **M**ontana.
This star 80s quarterback and three-time Super Bowl MVP led the 49ers to four Super Bowl victories. A pro at staying calm under pressure and making heart-stopping last-minute plays, 'The Comeback Kid' helped his teams to 31 fourth-quarter come-from-behind wins.

N is for Joe **N**amath.
His legendary prediction of the Jets-Colts game in Super Bowl III is still unforgettable: "We're going to win the game. I guarantee it." Appearing in many TV commercials during and after his NFL career, 'Broadway Joe' was not just a famous sports star – he was a pop culture icon.

O is for Otto Graham. Dominating the game in the 1950s, this legendary quarterback led the Cleveland Browns to 10 championship games in his 10 seasons with the team. Known as 'Automatic Otto' for his precision passes, his 8.63 yards per pass attempt is still an NFL record today.

P is for **P**eyton Manning. Laying down the law at the line of scrimmage, 'The Sheriff' became famous for calling out audibles just before the snap. With 14 Pro Bowl appearances, five MVP awards, and many other career records, this legend has certainly left his mark on NFL history.

Q is for Saquon Barkley. Leaving Penn State with a bunch of honors, Barkley was drafted by the Giants and went on to have a stellar rookie year. While not quite legend-status yet, Barkley represents the future of NFL legends to come.

R is for **R**eggie White.
Fulfilling his childhood dream
of becoming a football player
and a minister, the 'Minister
of Defense' was the best
defensive player in the NFL.
A two-time NFL sacks leader
who achieved a record
198 career sacks, this 6'5",
300 pound gentle giant
will never be forgotten.

S is for Barry Sanders. This four-time NFL rushing yards leader was ranked by the NFL Top 10 series as the "most elusive runner of all time." Breathtakingly fast and focused, 'Big Bad Barry' shunned the spotlight and played purely for the love of the game.

T is for Tom Brady.
With the most Super Bowl
wins, appearances, MVPs
and playoff wins, Brady
is considered the greatest
quarterback of his generation.
He famously brought the
Patriots back from the brink
to win their sixth Super
Bowl. Legendary!

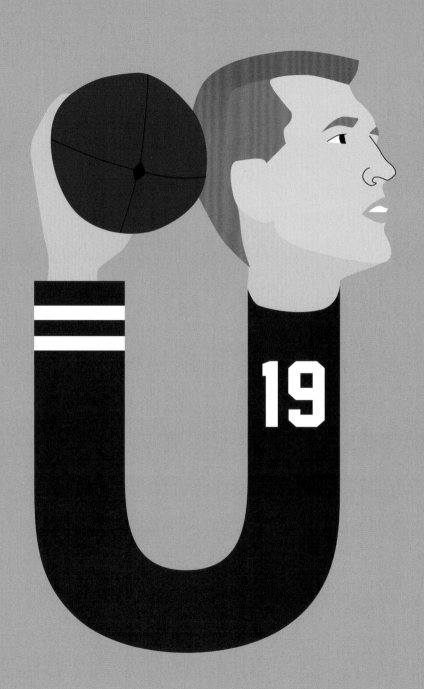

U is for Johnny **U**nitas.
In the 50s and 60s, 'Johnny U' set the bar high for what it meant to be a quarterback. Calling his own plays, every pass and decision he made was designed to win. His record of 47 consecutive games with at least one touchdown pass stood for over 50 years!

V is for **V**ince Lombardi. Super-coach Lombardi led the Green Bay Packers to six NFL championships and victory at the first two Super Bowls. He is considered to be the greatest coach in football history! No wonder they named the Super Bowl trophy in his honor.

W is for **Walter Payton.** Nicknamed 'Sweetness' for his kindness and running style, Payton was a record-setting running back and legendary human being. His legacy lives on in the Walter Payton NFL Man of the Year Award, presented every year to honor a player's volunteer and charity work.

Xx

X is for Dave Wilco**x**. Nicknamed 'The Intimidator,' this linebacker was physically and mentally suited to the role. Playing 11 seasons with the 49ers, he was named in the NFL All-Pro team five times and selected to play in seven Pro Bowls!

Y is for Steve **Y**oung. Brought in as a replacement for Joe Montana, the rivalry between these two brilliant quarterbacks was fierce. During his 13 seasons with the 49ers, Young was named MVP twice and he was also the MVP of Super Bowl XXIX.

Zz

Z is for Gary Zimmerman. This bulldozing yet humble offensive lineman led the Denver Broncos to their first Super Bowl win in 1997. Described by Pat Bowlen as the "John Elway of the offensive line," Zimmerman joined Elway in the Pro Football Hall of Fame in 2008.

The ever-expanding legendary library

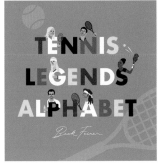

EXPLORE THESE LEGENDARY ALPHABETS & MORE AT WWW.ALPHABETLEGENDS.COM

FOOTBALL LEGENDS ALPHABET
www.alphabetlegends.com

Published by Alphabet Legends Pty Ltd in 2019
Created by Beck Feiner
Copyright © Alphabet Legends Pty Ltd 2019

UNICEF AUSTRALIA
A portion of the Net Proceeds from the sale of this book
are donated to UNICEF.

9 780648 506355